THE PEANUTS GANG LOVES TO DOODLE!

Create and Complete Full-Color Doodles
with Charlie Brown, Snoopy, and Friends

by Charles M. Schulz

RP|KIDS

PHILADELPHIA • LONDON

Books published by Running Press are available at special discounts for bulk purchases in the United States by corporations, institutions, and other organizations. For more information, please contact the Special Markets Department at the Perseus Books Group, 2300 Chestnut Street, Suite 200, Philadelphia, PA 19103, or call (800) 810-4145, ext. 5000, or e-mail special.markets@perseusbooks.com.

ISBN 978-0-7624-5093-0

9   8   7   6   5   4   3   2   1
Digit on the right indicates the number of this printing

Cover and interior design by Ryan Hayes and Frances J. Soo Ping Chow
Edited by Lisa Cheng
Typography: Typography of Coop

Running Press Kids
An Imprint of Running Press Book Publishers
A Member of the Perseus Books Group
2300 Chestnut Street
Philadelphia, PA 19103–4371

Visit us on the web!
www.runningpress.com/kids
www.snoopy.com

Watch out, Charlie Brown!
What is Lucy holding this time?

What did Sally receive in the mail?

Who is the subject of Snoopy's latest masterpiece?

Off to sea!
Decorate the sail and flag of Woodstock's boat.

Linus and Marcie found treasure on the way
to school! What does it look like?

What are Charlie Brown and
his friends selling at their stand?

Rerun is blowing lots of bubbles!
Doodle some big ones.

Give Spike a scenic place to picnic!
Fill the desert around him with cacti, rocks, and plants.

Draw lots of fluffy flakes for Snoopy to catch on his tongue. Remember, no two snowflakes are the same!

What is Charlie Brown looking for
in the cookie jar?

Poor Woodstock is all alone!
Draw some friends for his empty nest.

Breakfast looks yummy!
What are Linus and Lucy having?

Cowabunga! Draw Snoopy a snowboard.

What is Linus throwing for Snoopy to catch?

How is Charlie Brown's scarf decorated?

BOO!

Eek! What is scaring Charlie Brown?

Fall is in the air! Draw piles of leaves for
Snoopy and Woodstock to jump into.

What is Snoopy ready to catch?

What is Rerun drawing?

Lucy is playing doctor today! Who is coming
to see her? How much does she charge?

Nice toss, Charlie Brown!
Where is his Frisbee?

What does Snoopy see on his drive
through the country?

Schroeder is playing the piano,
but he needs some musical notes!

Caution! What kind of roadwork is being done?

What friends are watching TV with Charlie Brown, Snoopy, and Woodstock?

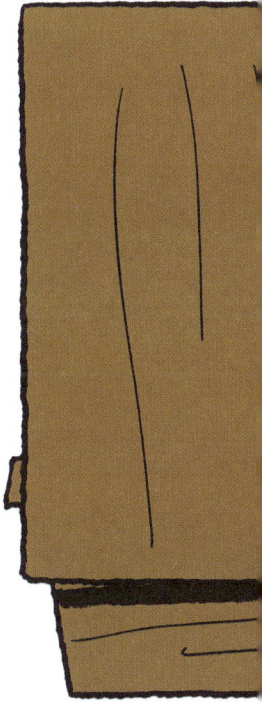

Marcie and Peppermint Patty are looking at a cool poster. What is on it?

What new land does the Flying Ace see?

Charlie Brown and Snoopy are daydreaming.
What kind of tree are they leaning against?

Will Snoopy use a raft or a bridge to rescue Woodstock? You decide!

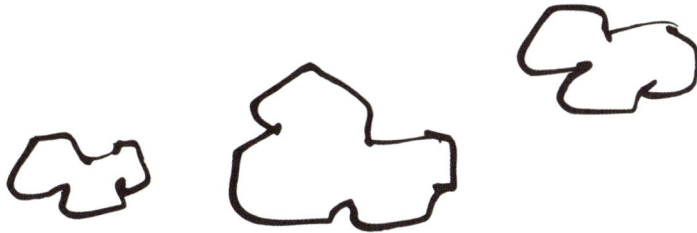

Snoopy rides his motorcycle through city streets.
Draw a skyline behind him.

What is chasing Charlie Brown?

Who is at the movies with Snoopy?

Decorate the flags that Woodstock and Snoopy are waving proudly.

Time to beat the heat!
Draw a place where everyone can go swimming.

Give Linus and Snoopy a trusty
blanket to snuggle with.

What does Snoopy see when he is in outer space?

Charlie Brown is unwrapping a present!
What's inside?

Make a wish! Finish the field of dandelions.

Who are driving the other Zambonis?

Decorate Snoopy's dream dog house.

What is Franklin catching?

Fore! Put some clubs in Charlie Brown's golf bag.

Where did that golf ball go?
And did Snoopy sink a hole in one?

Decorate Snoopy's sailboat as he sets out to sea!

Linus has found the Great Pumpkin!
What does it look like?

Show your troop pride!
What do the scouts' flags look like?

Draw a snowman for Snoopy
to hang the top hat on.

Charlie Brown is stranded!
Draw a boat to rescue him.

Ring, ring! Who is Lucy talking to?

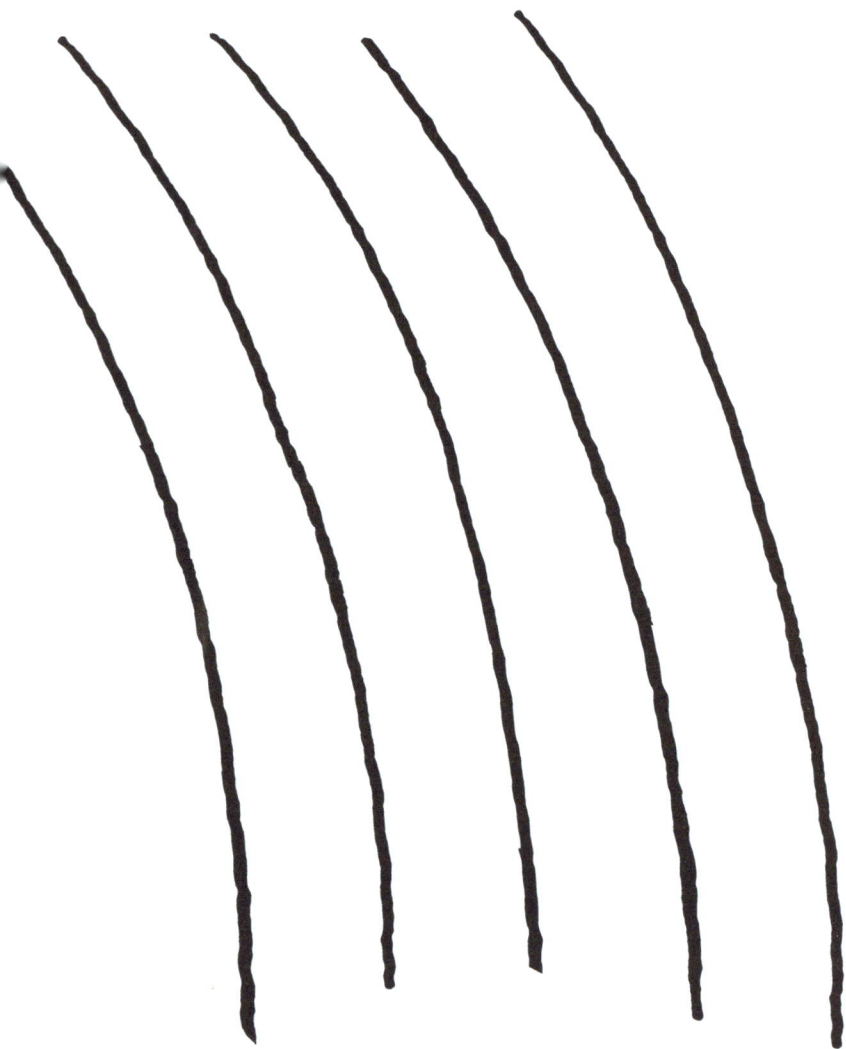

What does the pot at the end of the rainbow hold?

The Flying Ace wants to know what's for dinner.
Fill the table with your favorite foods.

What is Lucy giving Linus?

Are the fish biting for Woodstock and Snoopy?

What sights will Woodstock see
as he flies high in the sky?

Go fish! Draw Snoopy and Rerun
some cards so they can play.

Draw some lampshade hats
for Woodstock's friends.

Marcie and Peppermint Patty look chilly! Give them
a fire to warm their hands over.

All aboard the SS Snoopy!
Draw a boat for this canine captain.

Help Charlie Brown and Snoopy decorate the tree.

What is Sally carrying?

Peppermint Patty doesn't look too happy!
What's in the water?

What flag does this fearless leader wave?

What is Snoopy watering in his garden?

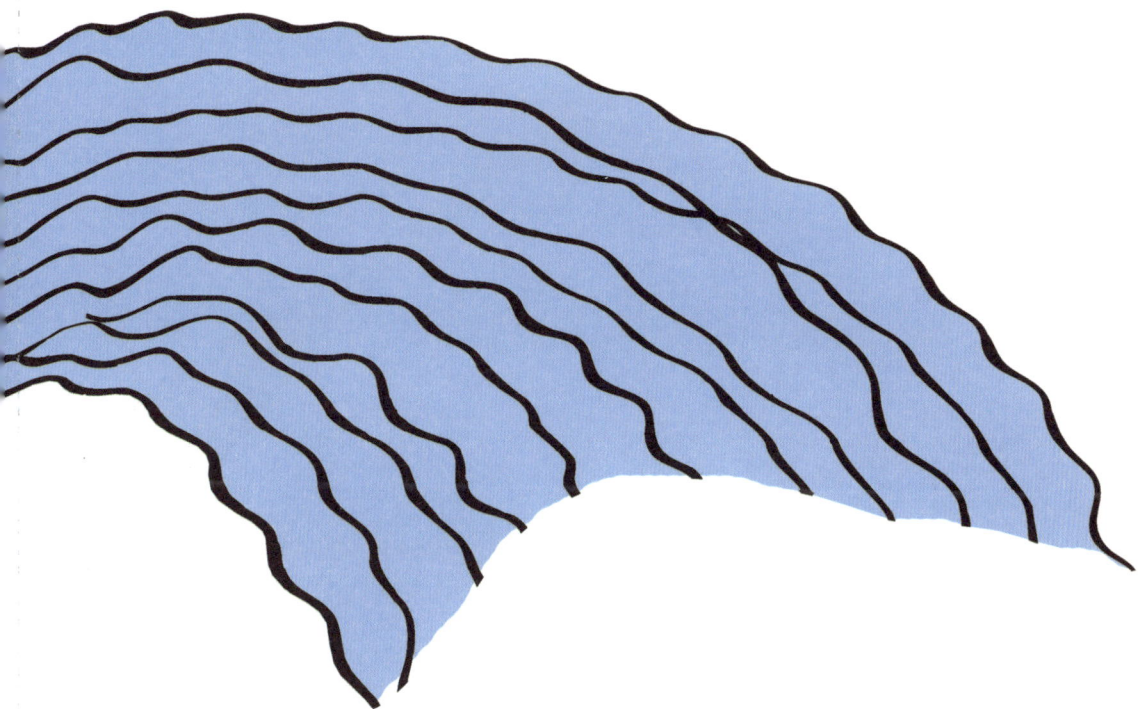

Draw a boat for Spike to row!

Linus and Sally built a sand castle.
What does it look like?

Snoopy dressed up as Santa Paws!
What is he carrying?

Linus's snowman needs some accessories! Doodle him some gloves, a hat, buttons, and a face.

Voilà! Complete Peppermint Patty's work of art.

Yum! What sort of food has chef Snoopy cooked?

Help Snoopy find water for his campers.

Do Snoopy, Woodstock, and their friends see
wild animals on the hike?

Make sure that Woodstock and his friends have all the gear they need for their camping trip.

What camping supplies did Snoopy pack in his bag?

Why is everyone waiting in line?
And what are they traveling with?

Peppermint Patty is in the mood for a snack.
What is she eating?

What kind of ball is Snoopy kicking?

Snoopy needs a piano to lean against
and music in the air. Help him out!

Finders keepers! What did Sally find
underneath the bed?

Draw Woodstock's musical instrument.

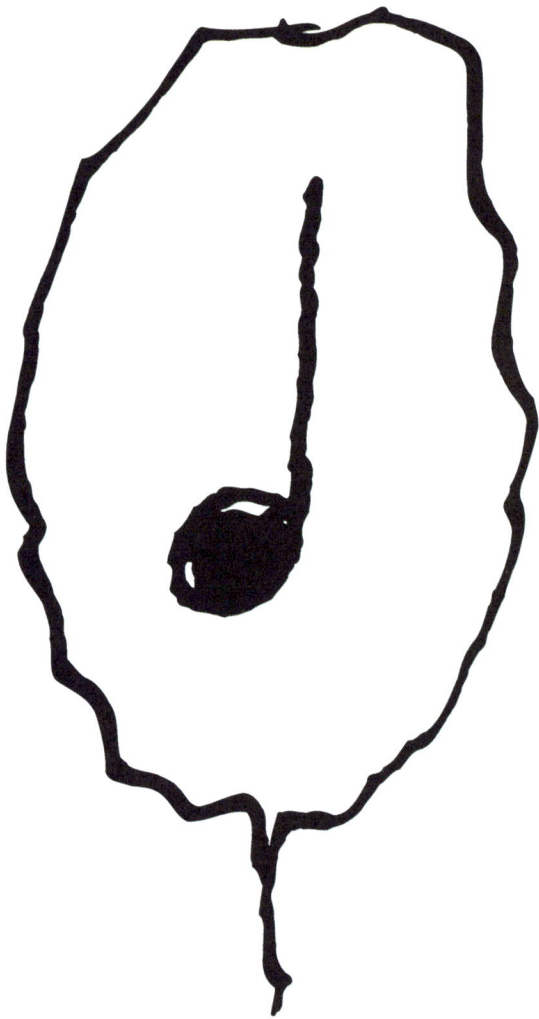

Snoopy's catching a wave!
Draw in some waves for Snoopy to ride.

Lucy and Linus are off to school! Give them backpacks, lunches, and anything else they need.

How did Snoopy carve his Jack O' Lantern?

Ahoy, matey! What do Snoopy and Woodstock see?

The Flying Ace and Peppermint Patty are out for a quick flight! What do they see up in the air?

What kind of treasure has
Snoopy and his pirate gang discovered?

What piece of artwork is Joe Cool showing off?

Lucy is being nice and giving Rerun a toy.
What is it?

Charlie Brown and Linus are on their way to school.
How will they get there?

What is Snoopy looking at
from the top of his dog house?

What is Charlie Brown holding that makes Snoopy so happy?

Woodstock is taking in the sun!
What does he need to stay cool?

Who is Charlie Brown sitting with on the couch?

Lucy can't catch the baseball!
Draw her a trusty glove.

Snoopy is practicing his poker face!
Who is he playing with?

Draw some trees and flowers that
Snoopy has planted.

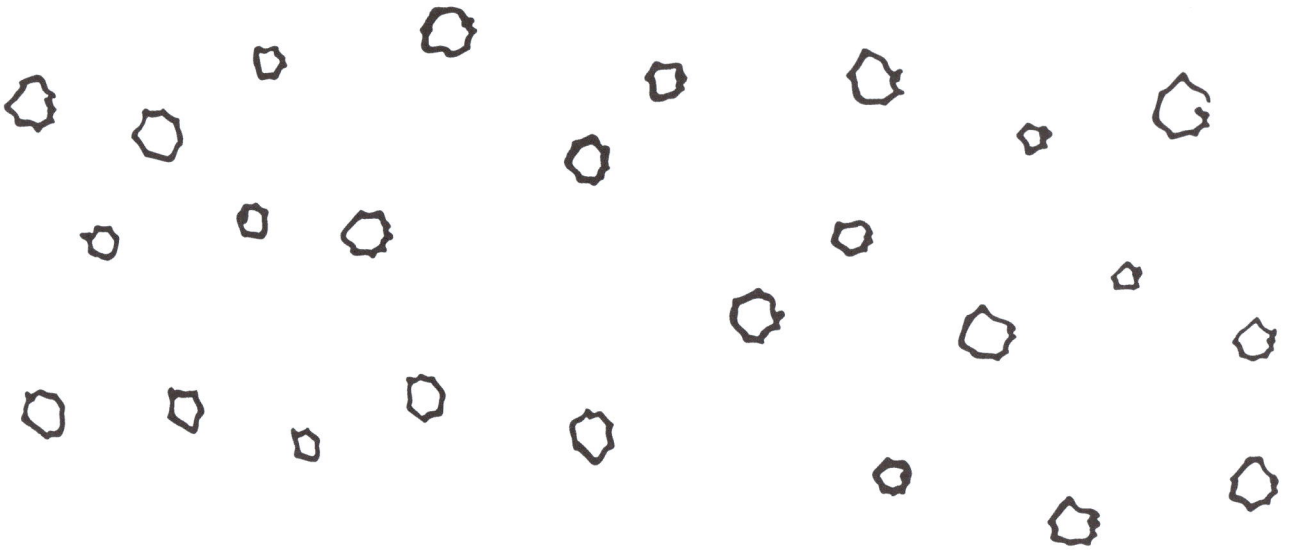

Let it snow! Finish this wintry scene.

Rerun wants to play! Give him a ball and a basket.

Make sure that there is a football
for Snoopy to catch!

Charlie Brown missed the ball again.
Maybe a hat will help him block out the sun.